Yo-Yo Tricks

Learn to Yo-Yo like a Pro – 125 Cool and Fun Basic to Professional Tricks

The Yo-Yo Prodigies

Table of Contents

Yo-Yo Tricks

Chapter 2: Something a Bit Trickier

Reverse trapeze

Pinwheel

Brain Twister

Skin the cat

Double or nothing

Reverse flip front mount

Chapter 3: Tricks to Impress the Whole Family

Split bottom mount

Barrel rolls

Atom smasher

Boing Boing trick

The motorcycle

Dog bite

Dog jumps through the hoop

Eating spaghetti

The sticky whip

Undermount

Overmount

Over and under

Brain Twister

Smashing the atom

Yo-Yo Tricks

Gunslinger

Assisted barrel rolls

Assisted Mach 5

Blue line mount

Incendio

Basic off string wind

Basic throw for off string

Toss and catch

Forward mount trick

Leg orbits

Underhand whip

Cast whip

Recaptures

String your counterweight

Hold the counterweight

360 trick

Release of the double or nothing

Chain Wraps

Arm wrap

Warp drive

The stall

Guillotine

Yo-Yo Tricks

© Copyright 2018 by The Yo-Yo Prodigies - All rights reserved.

The following eBook is produced below with the goal of providing information that is as accurate and reliable as possible. Regardless, purchasing this eBook can be seen as consent to the fact that both the publisher and the author of this book are in no way experts on the topics discussed within and that any recommendations or suggestions that are made herein are for entertainment purposes only. Professionals should be consulted as needed prior to undertaking any of the action endorsed herein.

This declaration is deemed fair and valid by both the American Bar Association and the Committee of Publishers Association and is legally binding throughout the United States.

Furthermore, the transmission, duplication, or reproduction of any of the following work including specific information will be considered an illegal act irrespective of if it is done electronically or in print. This extends to creating a secondary or tertiary copy of the work or a recorded copy and is only allowed with the express written consent from the Publisher. All additional rights reserved.

The information in the following pages is broadly considered a truthful and accurate account of facts and as such, any inattention, use, or misuse of the information in question by the reader will render any resulting actions solely under their purview. There are no scenarios in which the publisher or the original author of this work can be in any fashion deemed liable for any hardship or damages that may befall them after undertaking information described herein.

Additionally, the information in the following pages is intended only for informational purposes and should thus be thought of as universal. As befitting its nature, it is presented without assurance regarding its prolonged validity or interim quality. Trademarks that are mentioned are done without written consent and can in no way be considered an endorsement from the trademark holder.

Introduction

While many of us know the yo-yo as a toy that we played with when we were younger, it is widely believed that this is a device that comes from ancient China. The earliest depictions of the yo-yo are visible from other places throughout the world as well, with art showing these toys from Ancient Greece. At this time, they were often called discs because of the simple form of two discs that come from varying materials. In addition, the yo-yo has been mentioned through the Philippines, India, and Egypt.

Over time, the yo-yo started to make its appearance in France, looking very similar to how it did in ancient drawings and in other countries. Often a notable person of that society has been seen playing with or painted with the traditional yo-yo. Many members of the aristocracy at the time would want to follow the trend and the device would see a resurgence on occasion.

While it is believed that the yo-yo first gained popularity with the aristocracy of France during these times, it wasn't long until it spread through the upper classes of Europe, especially the English. As future kinds and other nobility started to play with these toys, it didn't take long before others of the upper classes clamored to get some of their own and the popularity of this toy was seen throughout that area.

Historically, the discs of the yo-yo were made out of some different materials including wood, porcelain, metal, and terracotta. While wood has long been seen as the more durable out of the materials, the others were often in demand to use during ceremonial or decorative purposes. For example, many porcelain yo-yos were found in China and terracotta dishes were popular in Ancient Greece.

Traditionally, the yo-yo had a short string that only allowed the two discs to move up and down. In the 1920s, the design of the string was changed. The Slip String was then introduced to help allow the yo-yo more freedom to do impressive tricks, which then allowed more flexibility with it and another rise in its popularity over time.

With the success of the Slip String, it soon became popular to try out new tricks to impress others and the United States held many contests to showcase the talents of fans throughout the country. Professionals soon emerged who would travel throughout the country to hold these contests, provide tips, and demonstrate sales to promote these toys even more.

Throughout time, competition in the best yo-yos started to come out. Many companies wanted to win the title of having the best product and more, but in 1969, the Flambeau Plastics

Company bought the Duncan name (Duncan was the main name of yo-yos and other popular toys in the decades prior). With this purchase, they also inherited the reputation that came with the older company and continued to produce yo-yos even to this day. The Flambeau Plastics Company did make some changes to the design of the yo-yo though. Previously, they were made out of maple wood, which made them the right density and weight for doing spins. But today, most of the products are made out of non-toxic K-resin plastic. In addition, the modern yo-yos now have a metal axel to make it easier to do the string with the toy without causing damage.

Many times, the yo-yo is seen as a little kid's toy, one that children will use a bit while outside and to get them away from the screen and video games. Many adults and older children may not consider using it because it is seen as a toy rather than something to be taken seriously. But this is about to change. As you will see with some of the tips and tricks that we will discuss in this guidebook, you will be able to take this simple device and turn it into a machine that can do a ton of different things for you.

The popularity of the yo-yo is starting to go up yet again. Many people are seeing that there is so much more to this device compared to just having it go up and down, and they are more excited than ever to learn some tricks that are new to them, can enhance their skills, and which can help them to really show off to others. This guidebook is going to show you the steps that you need to take your skills no matter where they currently are and move them to the next level to impress those around you.

Today, you are still able to find many competitions for yo-yos throughout the world. Most competitions will be split into two parts. You can find one part being compulsory tricks that you need to do and are set by the judges and then there is a freestyle section where you can do your own routine to impress the judges. You can find contests throughout the world including in France, China, Mexico, the UK, Japan, and America.

If you are looking to join a competition, then you will find the tools that you need in this guidebook. We will start out with some of the basic skills that you should know and that can get you out of the beginner stage into a more intermediate stage. And if you are looking to really impress at a competition and more, then you can easily use some of the tricks that are found in this guidebook to help you stand out from the crowd and do an amazing job overall.

Before we move into some of the different tricks that you can do when it comes to using the yo-yo, let's take a look at some fun facts that come with this great toy. These facts can make the use of a yo-yo so much more fun to use. Some of the facts that you can share with others as you show off all your new skills include the following:

- Yo-Yos have been around for a long time. In fact, art that was found that dated back to 500 BC in Ancient Greece showcase this toy.

- The modern yo-yo, the one that we now most associated with the toy, was patented in 1866. Charles Hettrich and James Haven were in charge of patenting this one. It was called the whirligig at the time.

- Competitions are found throughout the world for those who want to showcase their yo-yo skills.

- The word yo-yo means "come back" or "spring back" and comes from the Philippines.

- Japan is home to one of the most notable Yo-Yo world champions, Shinji Saito.

- You can get the yo-yo to spin for about twenty seconds. A beginner may have some trouble getting started with this and will need to practice. Having this spin and perfecting it can make a lot of the other tricks easier. If you want to get it to go or a bit longer than the twenty seconds, it may be worth your time to invest in a professional version of the yo-yo to help you get a better spin with your tricks.

- A professional grade yo-yo is able to spin a bit longer than the toy ones above. These can spin for between one to four minutes. But there is a world record that has the spin going for 21 minutes.

- All yo-yos are going to be composed of two cylindrical discs that are going to be connected together with an axle. The string will attach to this as well. And thanks to the longer string that has been developed, you will be able to do a lot of new tricks with the yo-yo, rather than just lifting it up and done.

Working with a yo-yo can be a great experience. You get the chance to work with a fun toy and learn a lot of great tricks. As you will learn in this guidebook, you will quickly find that it is easy to do even the most complicated of tricks and you can easily combine them together to get the best results possible. When you are ready to take your skills from beginner to expert and you want to be able to do tricks with one hand, two hands, combinations, and more, make sure to take a look through this guidebook to help you get started.

Chapter 1: Tricks for the Beginners

If you are brand new to the world of yo-yo-ing, it is time to begin with some of the basic tricks. These will help you to get familiar with the whole process and can make it easier as you advance to some of the other tricks that we will talk about later on. Some of the tricks that you can try out as a beginner includes:

Single loop the string

When you get started with the yo-yo, you will see that the basic string will have a knot at the end and then the other end is attached to the yo-yo. To do this, grasp the string at the end and again about an inch lower. Untwist the string and you will start to see a loop appear. Put your middle finger and thumb in the opening and then place over the yo-yo. Allow this to twist again so that the

21

string is holding onto the center. This is a single loop and you will want to do this as you put the yo-yo together or you will get the string caught up and it is hard to fix later.

Double looping the string

To start this one, use the method that we talked about above. With that method, you are going to have a yo-yo that is set up to do a lot of great tricks that can go above what a beginner can do. You can re-do the loop again to help change the sensitivity so it is easier to do the easier tricks. We can switch back to the single loop later on when we are ready for some of the more advanced tricks.

Adjusting the height of the string

The height of the string is going to be different for each person. The ideal length here is determined by extending the forearm from your waist and then letting the string fall to just above the level of the floor. Or you can hold the yo-yo between your feet and bring the string up to your belly bottom. Loop the string over your finger and you have the perfect length for the yo-yo. Cut off the string that is left over and then get started.

Winding the string

In the traditional method, you will hold the yo-yo and then manually wind the string around the spool. This works just fine but can take up a lot of time and is boring. To learn this trick, we need to first understand what makes the yo-yo wind up. First, it needs to be spinning with the line slack. To make the machine wind up automatically, you need to make sure that it is spinning and then drop your hand fast to make the slack. This is going to make the yo-yo wind back to your hand on its own!

The basic throw

The first thing that you need to learn here is the basic throw. To make sure that you hold the yo-yo the proper way, hold the palm out and set the device on the hand. Have the string go over the top of it. This is the best way for you to hold onto the device for this throw. From here, you just throw the yo-yo off your hand and then when the string gets to the bottom, you just pull it back up by turning the hand over. Try this a few times and you will get the hang of bringing the yo-yo up and down.

The sleeper

When a yo-yo is considered sleeping, it is going to spin right at the end of the string. A common mistake when mastering this kind of trick is that you will do too hard of a throw the first time. This can create some slack that can make it

24

hard to get the yo-yo to stay put. With this slack, the yo-yo wants to go right back up. To help yourself stop this effect, you need to do some compensation for the bounce with a bit of cushion. Practice moving your hand so that it goes up and down just a little bit. This can take some practice to find the exact movement that will work for you. Once you get this motion ready, you will be able to get the yo-yo to sleep no matter how hard you are throwing it.

Walk the dog

This is a very popular trick for the yo-yo out there and you will be surprised at how easy it is to learn this one. First, you need to throw out a strong sleeper before laying this on the ground. The momentum that is caused when the yo-yo spins is going to make the device look like it is walking with you on the ground, either in front of you or behind you.

There are two tips that you can use with this one that makes the trick more impressive than before. First, you should never have the operating hand go too close to the yo-yo. This is going to create some slack and can make the yo-yo come back. Second, a bit of swing backward before you lay the device on the ground can add in some momentum and the yo-yo is going to end up moving faster for this trick.

The creeper

This is a great option to work with after Walk the dog because you just extend out the movement that you mastered there. Here, you are going to walk forward as you did in the previous trick, but then you just kneel down and get the yo-yo back to the hand, while it is still on the ground. This one is not too difficult for a beginner to master, you just need to throw a strong sleeper, propel the yo-yo so it goes ahead of you, and then you need to get it to come back to your hand and you have finished your creeper.

Around the corner

This is a trick that will involve the sleeper. Get the yo-yo over into the sleeper and then lift it up with the back of your arm. From here, you can give a gentle tug on the device so that it comes back to you. Then throw the device over your shoulder before making it come back to your hand. If you are working with a device that has an auto-return function, then it will be able to do a lot of the work for you, but for a conventional yo-yo, you just need to use the tug, throw, and pull actions that we just discussed.

The elevator

The next trick that we are going to take a look at is the elevator. The key to doing this kind of trick is to give off the illusion that the device is going up the string. This may sound a bit complicated, but even a beginner is able to figure it out. You just need to throw the yo-yo, make sure that it gets stuck on the string, and then pull apart the hands.

The key to getting success out of this trick is to have your bottom hand a little in front of the top hand. This will help prevent the yo-yo from bouncing off the string, which can spoil the illusion that you are going for. Then, when you are ready, you can take the bottom hand and put it right above the second hand before pulling them apart. Then, when you reach the top, throw the yo-yo up a little and take the finger out. After you have been able to do this, you will find that the device comes right back and the elevator is mastered.

Rock the baby

With this trick, the string is going to make a picture when you are done. There are different types of picture tricks that you can do and a handy thing to remember is to practice doing these kinds of tricks with the device hanging, without it spinning. This makes it easier for you to get the string to behave the way that you want while creating the picture.

To create the illusion of rocking the baby with your yo-yo, you just need to throw the device, grab with the other hand right in the middle of the string. From here your hand needs to go right under the yo-yo and point out two fingers. This is going to create a cradle effect. Rock the baby here a few times before dropping the yo-yo. Provided that you still have a little bit of spin to the device, you will get the slack that is needed to get the device back in your hands.

Eiffel Tower

Another one of the picture tricks that you can work on is the Eiffel Tower. This is a good one to use when you can stop the spinning of the yo-yo. Take your opposite hand and use it to pull right into the string. Use the yo-yo hand to lay over the top of this, with the thumb of that hand lifting the string and taking the opposite hand, twist it back towards yourself and that will cross the string.

From here, take the first finger and grab the string before pulling the string through the loop that was just created. Allow the remainder of the string to fall off your opposite hand. The point of doing this is to lead the string just being on the first finger of the opposite hand and the thumb of your yo-yo hand. For the last part of this, you can take the ring finger and yo-yo finger and then use them to twist forward and make sure that the string is pinched in between them.

At this point, you will be able to see the shape of the tower that you are trying to create.

You can take the time to shape it a little bit here if you would like. Once you have this one down, you can increase the speed and then get a better shape of the tower.

Forward toss

Now we are going to start working with a looping yo-yo trick. You need to start out with a forward throw of the yo-yo in order to get started. Throw the yo-yo and then when it has come halfway back to you, push the yo-yo hand on top of the toy in order to get it to flip over. You can work on flipping the hand as well as the toy to get a bit more control when you get to the more advanced moves. Just like with our basic throw, make sure that the string is in the right position over the device because this one is not going to work the way that you want with the device upside down.

31

When you are ready to do the forward toss, you can throw the yo-yo so it is underhand and then turn your hand so it is able to catch the device. Swing your hand right by the side and then when you are halfway through this motion, let go. The momentum from this swing should help give you the power that you need but if you see that it doesn't come back up as you need, you are either letting the device go too later or too early. This is definitely a move that needs some good timing so practice it a bit and you will see success.

Visiting Grandma

To get this trick to work, you will need to use the forward toss and the basic loop. The difference with this trick is that the device needs you to put it to sleep before it goes all the way around the world. When you attempt to get this kind of motion to work, you will find that throwing the device into the distance can help you get the right amount of momentum. And if the spinning of the device is still going, then you can do this same movement a few times.

Riding the elevator 2

To start this trick, you can throw the yo-yo and then take a finger from the free hand under your string, pulling the device up. When the device is raised, you will land the gap of the device on your string, the one held by the throwing hand, before pulling the hands a bit apart. This gives the impression that your device is going up the string.

Throw the baby

To perform this trick, you need to master rock the baby that we talked about above. While you rock the baby, you move the fingers that are pinching the string together away to the side. From here, you can spin the device to yourself several times before you throw it in the air and get it to return to you.

The Texas Star

This is another picture trick that can be really great. It is going to be done with just the throwing hand. To perform the star, you need to bring the thumb up under the string and then lift it a bit. From here, you can then wrap the string around the ring finger then wrap it around the little finger followed by the thumb and middle finger. Then spread the fingers apart and you will have a nice star shape here.

Texas Double Star

This is a variation of the trick above that is going to use both of your hands. To begin, just let the yo-yo hang a bit. Then take the thumb of the free hand and pull the string across. Use the ring finger of the dominant hand to pull it back into a V shape. With your free hand, take the pointer finger and have it lift up the remaining string to get it to

34

hang off and the device will be at the front of the star. With the thumb of the dominant hand, you can pull the remaining hanging string back through the largest space in the star. To finish, you can pull the middle finger of your dominant hand down in front of your star and use it to lift up the remaining string. This should make the star shape that you want.

The cross

This one is similar to the Eiffel Tower but takes a little bit different approach. To begin, you let the device hang down and then use the free hand to help lift up the string. Then use the thumb of your throwing hand to help lift up the string. Twist around the free hand to form the 8. Next, don't allow the string time to fall from the hand, but let it hang from both of your thumbs as well as the pointer finger of the free hand. Then finish this with a pinch of the string together to form your cross.

35

The Rattlesnake

To do the rattlesnake, you can throw a sleeper sideways. Allow it to have some time to spin in its side. Then bring the free leg so it goes against the string. You should hear a sound like a rattle. That is the rattlesnake. Pull the device back up when you are done.

Shooting the moon

This is another fun trick that you can try out when you are ready to enhance your skills a little bit. To do this one, you need to throw the device and then swing the wrist into a kind of semi-circle so that the device ends up going above your head. As it begins to fall a bit, snap the device so it goes in front of you. And then, as it returns again, flick the device upwards. Repeat this as many times as you want but be very careful not to hit yourself.

The tunnel

To get started with the tunnel, you will get started with an around the world. As the yo-yo starts to fall down in front of you, you can spread out the legs a bit and then let the device swing right through them. After swinging the device, you can allow it to roll itself back out and up into your hand to finish the trick.

The elephant

Another trick that you may want to work with is the elephant. To get started with this one, you can set up a light chair so it is sitting right in front of you. When you are ready, throw a hard and fast sleeper that goes right in front of you. Then allow the yo-yo to just swing over the chair while it continues to spin. This will be the trunk of the elephant. Tug back up to end the trick or to get it to restart.

37

The pickpocket

The next trick that you can work with is known as the pickpocket. To do this trick, you will need to use your free hand to open up the pocket at that time as wide as you possibly can. When you are ready, you will need to throw a hard sleeper. As the yo-yo starts to spin, allow it to spin between your legs a little bit. With a bit of practice and with a sleeper that is hard enough, you will be able to get the yo-yo to land right in that open pocket with the throw.

Finger spinning

This trick is going to be a bit different compared to some of the other ones we have looked at so far. To begin this finger spin, you will need to throw the yo-yo so that it goes in the opposite direction of your body, rather than having it go across on the finger. You will also want to catch it with your non-throwing hand rather than

38

with the throwing hand. The throwing hand needs to maintain some tension in the string and can help you get out of the trick as needed. To start, you can throw the device so it goes at a slight angle. Then catch the cupped side with your finger before bringing that finger down a bit allowing for some more control over the spin.

The tsunami

This is another one where you will begin by throwing a sleeper. When you are in the sleeper, you can bring the string over so it is on the index finger of your throwing hand. Then swing the device to repeat this over the same finger but on the non-throwing hand. You can finish this trick by swinging the device back to the throwing hand and then grab the yo-yo.

Eli Hop

For this trick, you can start out by getting into a trapeze. You can snap the yo-yo up before taking the two hands and bringing them close together. As the device starts to come back to you, take the throwing hand away from the free hand so that the device can land itself right on the trapeze. You can continue doing this trick as many times as you would like, following the same instructions or move on to the next trick.

Yo-Yo Tricks

Chapter 2: Something a Bit Trickier

Now that you have learned a few of the simple tricks of using the yo-yo and have gained some familiarity that comes with this kind of device, it is time to take those skills and enhance them to do a bit more than before. Some of the intermediate tricks that you can use once you have gotten the basics down include:

Introduction to looping

You need to have a good grasp on doing the forward toss before the loop can be successful. When you get the yo-yo spinning and it reaches the spot in front of your hand, you can bend the wrist so it goes backward and then do a flip with the device. When you do this trick on the inside of the wrist, you only need to have that motion with your wrist and the right kind of timing to make this work. You may need to experiment with your timing a little bit before you are able to get this one. This is the inside loop so experiment a bit to get it right before moving on.

Outside loop

This is another loop that you can do. The outside wrist loop is a bit more complicated, but you simply go with the same movements as the loop above but you will add in some movement from your elbow and shoulders as well. This can make the loop more energetic, so use a bit of control to make sure that you can maintain the loop and that it doesn't hit you along the way. Do an angle with this one to help you get the control that you want.

UFO

This is also known as the Sleeping Beauty trick. It is a great trick to learn to impress others and can help you adjust any strings that have become a bit twisted when you start practicing. Instead of throwing the yo-yo device so that it goes down, you will throw it over to your left. Then grab the string with the other hand as it gets to the end. Pull up the string so that the device starts to tilt over to one side.

In normal tricks, this is a disaster because you don't want a tilt. But this trick needs the tilt. Once the yo-yo has been able to turn a few times, it will be horizontal with a vertical spin and this will untwist the string. Once the string is unwound enough, then you can pull it up and release. The device is going to keep going upwards. If the string does need more untwisting, then just repeat the motion. You must perform this trick with a responsive yo-yo.

Fence hop

Now it is time to hop the fence. To do this, throw the yo-yo down and when it comes back up and is at the halfway point, you can push the yo-yo hand over the device and this causes it to do a little flip. If you are worried about having more control over this, you can flip the hand a bit. This can be a good one to help you with more complicated tricks later on.

Loop the loop

This is a good trick that is going to help you show off some of your skills and can give off the idea that the yo-yo is on more of an elastic band instead. You will start with a forward pass, making sure that the yo-yo goes forward. As it does this, the yo-yo will rotate and then sleep for a bit before returning back to you. But instead of catching the device, you can bring the hand down and swing the yo-yo over and then around it. This is going to make the device go the other way and it will flip over. Repeat this and flip the device again and

45

again as many times as you would like. Once this is done, you can catch the device and the trick finishes!

Three leaf clover

This is the trick you will use in order to create a three-leaf clover. You can do this by looping the first throw upwards at an angle of degrees. Then the second throw will stay at a level and then the final throw will be downward, going at a 45-degree angle.

Flips

Flips are going to be the opposite of what we are doing with loops. The flip is going to be done with two movements that are opposite from each other. If you throw the yo-yo to the ground and then flip it forward and then backward in order to get a flip. The motion that you use is going to depend on which direction the device is going.

Breakaway

This trick is going to help you throw the device across your body now. You can practice throwing it normally and then you just need to twist your hand a bit to the right. This makes the yo-yo go parallel to the body. When you twist the hand back, you can catch that device between your thumb and the rest of your hand. You can then just twist the device around in the direction that works the best for you to finish this move.

The man on the flying trapeze

This is an extension of the breakaway that we just talked about and it helps you to do that trick better and see different results. To get this trick to work, you need to take the alternative hand and its first finger and keep it rigid. As soon as the string touches that first finger, you just need to move the hand away and then move it back to the finger after the device is able to land on the string.

47

You need to move the hand back to quicken up how fast the string moves as it goes on your finger, which can make the action of landing on the string easier. To get the device to come back to you, you can give it a bit of slack and pull both of the hands apart. Then throw that device into the air while releasing the loop that is on your free hand. The yo-yo will wind and come back to be caught with your throw hand.

Reverse trapeze

Once you have gotten down the trapeze, you can work with the reverse trapeze. To do this one, pop the yo-yo as normal when you are ready to do the dismount. But instead of releasing the loop, you want to pinwheel the yo-yo around the free hand and then direct it towards the bottom of the string. Once the string is hit, you can let some slack come in and the yo-yo will pull the string over to the opposite hand. Then watch for the device to roll over to the freehand. You can wind up the excess string and snag it.

Pinwheel

The trapeze can be the beginnings of this next trip. Once you have been able to achieve it and the yo-yo starts to pass underneath, you can pinch on the string and get it to open back up. This allows the device to continue the same motion underneath. At this point, you are doing the Pinwheel.

Brain Twister

Use the same starts as the Trapeze, but then point the finger to the right and leave it there. Throw your yo-yo and once it is in a good swing, you want to throw it forward. When it comes back,

49

pull up your hand and then let it drop down so that the yo-yo lands right on the string. This is known as a good mount and once it is done, take the finger that is on the yo-yo and push it. You can use the free hand to keep this motion going. It is normal if the string does go around the finger a bit.

Skin the cat

To start with this trick, throw out a fast sleeper so it is in front of you. Then take the middle finger on your free hand and glide it up the string so it reaches your yo-yo finger. Lift the free hand a bit while tugging on the string backward until you get six inches from the opposite hand. Then flip it up with your finger and tug back with your yo-yo hand. Do not catch it here, but go into a forward pass so that the device is able to fly in front of you. When it returns, you can catch the device.

Double or nothing

To start this trick, begin with the breakaway and give the device some time to swing to the free hand. Then let the string go around your finger. You can move the hand a bit away and let the string go up, rather than doing a landing like the trapeze. Once it descends, you can let the string start to wrap around the index finger of the hand that holds onto the device. Once it is wrapped up, the string can loop the free hand again and then the device needs to land on the central string, forming a small free-falling trapeze.

Reverse flip front mount

You can start this one with a front mount. Then swing the device so it goes forward, pulls down a bit with the yo-yo hand and then the device is going to flip backward for you.

Chapter 3: Tricks to Impress the Whole Family

Now that you have some of the basics of using the yo-yo and some of the simple tricks started, we are going to start moving into turning some of these tricks into a performance that you can do in front of family and friends. Some of the tricks that you can do here include:

Split bottom mount

This trick is a good one to get started with here. To start, you can throw a sleeper. Then take the index finger of your opposite hand while bringing the hand with the device down. Then press the index finger of this hand into the string and move the device onto the front of the string. Now, take the left hand and lower it to make a loop that can frame everything and this trick is done.

Barrel rolls

You can do this trick by starting the split bottom mount. But you need to make some adjustments to your hands so you have an underpass with the free hand. Then bring this hand back up. You can do the same movement with the hand holding the device. What is going to show up here looks like an underpass and you are actually looping the yo-yo over the index finger before landing it back into the split bottom mount. You can keep doing this and each time the string is going to wrap itself around the index finger.

Atom smasher

This is another one that needs the split bottom mount as a start. Start with that trick and create a nice underpass with the yo-yo, ensuring that the working hand is the one that is on the front. The other hand needs to move into the double string before switching with your yo-yo hand. You should

53

have a nice underpass then when you move the hand under the device. Then flip the device into a somersault and the Atom smasher is done.

Boing-Boing trick

Start out again with the split bottom mount and start making it look like a barrel roll but instead of moving the device forward, you can let the working hand drop down and then have it back up again. The device is going to head to you and when it touches the other string, you can let the hand that has the yo-yo lower down to finish.

The motorcycle

This trick can start out with a fast sleeper. When you get that far, grab the string between the thumb and the front finger stay about 8 inches from the hand that has the yo-yo. Your free hand needs to raise the string higher than the yo-yo and use the other hand's thumb and middle finger to grab the string. The free hand can be released so that it will reach through the new loop and pull through the string so you end up with the handles of the motorcycle. From here, you can lower the device all the way to the floor. This makes it appear to travel along the ground and you are holding the handlebars.

Dog bite

To do this one, you can throw a fast sleeper again and have your legs near to 20 inches apart. Then swing the device so it goes between your legs, going just below knee length. Do a quick pull on the string so the device is able to grab the fabric of your pants, but you need to be able to plan this right. This then makes it look like the device is biting your leg.

Dog jumps through the hoop

You can take the dog bite one a bit further with this trick. Start by walking the dog, but rather than letting the device walk in front of you, you can place it behind the leg, the one that is on the same side as the device that holds the device. Now, form a hoop by taking your hand to your waist with the elbow perpendicular to the ground. You can control the dog by tugging on the string and swinging the yo-yo behind and through this hoop.

Eating spaghetti

Start this trick with a hard sleeper and then pull up bunches of string. Hold this bunches in your fist. Drop the strings and then finish the effect by wiping your mouth and then catch the yo-yo with a flashy catch.

The sticky whip

You can get started with this trick by throwing your sleeper. Then, turn the hand so that the palm is facing to the left (you will want to do this version with your right hand, though you can do the opposite and do it with the left hand if you choose). Allow the string to hang right over the thumb. Then snap it forward so you get a loop of a string that is able to fall into the gap, which can cause the yo-yo to hang.

Undermount

For this one, you can create a sleeper, but make sure that you throw it so the sleeper is away from the body. Bring out the index finger of the non-throwing hand so it goes under the string. Then use the throwing hand to pull down a bit, raising up the yo-yo so it has a chance to swing to you. Swing this into the string and then bring it so the hand is up around the yo-yo.

Overmount

To start with the overmount, you are going to do the opposite of what you did with the undermount. Pull your index finger, the one on your throwing hand back against the string. This will help you to get the yo-yo to be up on the string. Then loosen the hold of the throwing hand to get a swing going with the device. Keep swinging until the device ends up going into the loop.

Over and under

This one will need you to get through the undermount. Then, when you are towards the end, you can swing the device so it gets out of the undermount. Allow the yo-yo to swing up and then go around the ring or the middle finger (you choose which is easier) and then move it into the overmount. And then the device needs to go back into the undermount. Go back and forth with these two movements as many times as you would like before ending.

Yo-Yo Tricks

Brain Twister

To work on the brain twister, you will need to start the yo-yo out with an undermount. When you are finishing up the undermount, you can pull out the free hand and put it over the throwing hand. Then pull the throwing hand back so it is against the string and upwards to help sling the yo-yo. Sling this device over the throwing hand before swinging it down.

Smashing the atom

For this one, you need to do the split bottom mount. Then move the dominant hand so that it ends up under the yo-yo. From here, move the free hand so that it is on a double string before swapping the hands around. Then take the throwing hand and bring it under the device. Flip this a bit similar to what you did with the brain twister. Continue doing this as many times as you would like before grabbing the device again.

Houdini Mount

For the Houdini mount, this is similar to the double or nothing but you will continue to go around your thumb rather than the finder. This allows you to unhook your thumb there and can place you back in the Trapeze. If you would like to make this more impressive, you can unhook the thumb right when it hits on the string and then everything drops into it.

Zipper

To start with this one, you want to get into the basic front mount and then get right off. Doing this gets the device to swing forward a bit. Then you can use your middle finger to intercept the string and make sure that the device gets back onto the string on the opposite side. Do this again to get it back onto the opposite side again. From here, you will take the throwing hand and go right to the front of everything. Then roll up the yo-yo before going back to the first finger, helping you get into the same mount again.

Halley's Comet

This trick is basically going to combine the Man on the Flying Trapeze and the One-handed star tricks that we talked about before. You can combine both of these together to get a nice comet trick that will impress others. You can go back and forth between these two tricks to see what works the best for you and to really impress those around you.

Skin the Gerbil

This is going to include a bunch of the tricks that we already know, with a few new elements that have been added in and it can be a great one if you are trying to show off or do a little show. To start this one, you will throw a trapeze and then do a few forward flips before landing into the double trapeze. Flip this off and you will be back into the trapeze. Now, you can do a double trapeze over the throwing hand and flip off again to get back into the trapeze. From here, you can go back over the opposite hand, similar to doing a double trapeze again but you want to miss in front, swing again, land on the string, and then unwind and bring it back to your hand.

Ripcord

To begin this one, you will want to do a mount of one and a half mount and then a split bottom mount. What you will see is that in the front of this there will be one single string and then a double string behind it. All that you need to do now is roll the device onto that double string, doing this twice. During the second time, you will let go of the string that is on the throwing hands first finger. This sets you back up to the trapeze mount. You may then want to go from here over to either a side mount or a front mount.

Pops Yo-Yo Trick

Pops is another simple trick that can look amazing. You can choose to do it from a variety of mounts, but the easiest way is the Houdini Mount. Essentially, what you want to do is dismount and then re-mount again. You can do this a few times while sliding the loop from your finger and then pulling it back on. Try it from a few different mounts and see what it looks like.

Ninja Vanish

This is a type of Green Triangle trick and you will want to get started with it by throwing a breakaway. From here, you will then want to stick a finger under the string before pinching. From here, you can pop up the device. This gives you some slack. You can then whip this behind the string and create a loop so that you can whip it right into the yo-yo before catching it. From there, you can be back in a Green Triangle in order to pop right out of the front.

The Gondola

The key to doing this trick is that you are going to throw a double or nothing. But rather than throwing it around the first finger of the non-throwing hand like normal, you would throw it around the thumb and then around the first finger. Once you have this going, you can pinch the string using the throwing hand. Drop the string from the thumb, spin the string around before looping it across the opposite pointer finger. From here, you can pinch the string before pulling it through from there so you can move it to the right. Now, drop the string all the way off the throwing hand and slide it to the left before dropping the string out to finish.

Chapter 4: A Little Bit of the Fancy Stuff

This chapter is going to move on to some more impressive tests, ones that will take the knowledge that you have from the other chapters and make them into something bigger and new. We will start out with some of the slack string tricks that can help you to make more loops and create a different effect than you can get with the taut strings from before. Some of the different tricks that you can do here include:

Slack trapeze

To start this trick, pinch the string with your opposite hand so you create a bit of slack between this pinch and the throwing hand. Then flip this slack so it goes up and over the wrist of the other hand. Now, throw this down and ensure that one strand stays in that gap. Once you get it caught, make sure that the string is taut and then swing up the yo-yo over the opposite hand. From here, you can pinwheel around the working hand to make a Trapeze. Then go around the throw hand or you will get extra winding in that gap.

Reverse slack trapeze

The reverse direction of the trick above is another trick you can learn. Begin with a classic trapeze like we talked about above and then pinch with the free hand. The working hand needs to throw the string down quickly while throwing a loop of string under the opposite wrist. From here, circle the wrist a second time so that the pinch is caught in your gap. When this happens, you can pull the string taut to get a dismount as you did with the double or nothing.

Hidemasa hook

This is a whip trick that is similar to the one that we did above but without the pinch from before. To do this one, throw a breakaway and then hang the device for a bit before jerking it upwards and whipping the string down under the non-working hand's index finger. The device needs to hover next to the finger and the string should continue going around the finger so it slips into the gap. Allow the string to have time to get caught there before pulling the string tight. This lets the device rest in that loop. You can dismount this one by swinging the device over your opposite hand.

Side style back bind

As you come out of the Hidesema hook, you can work on this next trick. You can allow the string to get caught on your finger and then move it around and up your string. A little slack should be allowed here and then let the device go along

68

with it, without the free hand catching it here. From here, try the reverse trapeze before moving on.

Plastic whip

This is a trick that you can do with a device that is unresponsive. You will begin this one with a hard sleeper and then you can follow it by using the holding hand in the shape of a Y, with your palm facing the left-hand side. The string should be running over the thumb and the finger before you throw your hand forward to make a loop. The loop needs to hand down so the device can hang off the string that is looped over your fingers here.

Suicide

To work with this trick, you can throw a breakaway and then go through the trapeze. Take your free hand and place it under the hand working the device. You can release a loop with a flick of the finger. When the loop is released, do a circular motion in the front of the device hand. When you get close to your original position, you can slip a finger through this loop to make it easy to catch the suicide loop.

Iron Whip

The key to getting this trick to work is to make sure that the tension of the string stays consistent. Then start out with the trapeze and use the string out of this move in order to create an open loop. While you are holding the loop, you want to get the device to move towards you. Use the gap to help whip the loop down and then return back to the original position that comes with the trapeze. Then catch the device to end this trick.

Wave slack

To begin this trick, you can do a breakaway and then move on to the trapeze. Then you can pinch the string with your free hand and create a bit of under slack using the working hand. Alternate the slack and your device just by swinging the slick while the device is spinning around. This movement can be maintained by releasing and then re-catching the string. This makes some momentum until you are ready to land a trapeze to finish the trick.

Kwyjibo

This is a trick that is going to need a few dismounts and pops to make it work. You will start out with a pop up from the trapeze and then you can do a crossover with your device hand over the other hand onto the string. Roll it over to a mount before crossing to the working hand underneath to end up with a double or nothing. To get this trick done, you can do another pop and land in the trapeze position.

71

The Yo-Yo Prodigies

One and a half side mount

Start out with a strong breakaway and let it pass over your other hand before having it go over the working hand. Then it needs to land on the string that is farther away from you. You may want to stop the motion and take the time to control momentum by swinging the yo-yo.

Buddha's revenge

Start this trick from the previous trick. For this trick, you can take your hands and cross them making sure that you don't give any slack to the device at the same time. A slack string will make this not work well because the yo-yo will head back to you. Once your hands are crossed, all that you need to do is place both of the hands under the yo-yo so that it lands right on the string. When this trick is done the right way, you will end up back in the one and a half side mount. You can then go back through and repeat this trick as much as you want.

Cold fusion

To get ready for this trick, start out in the double or nothing. Then take both of the hands so they are under the yo-yo and land it on the string. You can then push the strings a bit so the device is on the outside string. Remove a finger here so you have a one and a half mount again. Once you are at this point, the trick just needs you to pass the opposite hand over all of this and bring it back to end up with a double twist. To dismount from this, unwrap everything twice and pull it over as the device comes off the string.

Mach 5

This is a trick that provides you with the illusion that your device is floating while your hands keep moving in a circle. Start out this trick with a split bottom mount and then create an underpass with the non-throwing hand so that you pass under the yo-yo. Then go back up so the throwing hand ends up between the device and the other hand. From here, remove the free hand so it will appear that the yo-yo is suspended there between the hands. Keep rotating the hands as many times as you would like. To finish this trick, have the free hand the farthest away from you and then close the hands together, removing the index finger to close it up.

Wrist mount

This is going to be similar to the double or nothing but you will use the wrist and then land on a middle string. You can begin with the double or nothing and then let the yo-yo fly over the wrist on your throwing hand. Then use the other hand and have the index finger wind up the device. Land the device on the middle string that comes from the base of the wrist. When you do this, you have finished the wrist mount.

Dice grinds

To start with this trick, you can throw the yo-yo so it goes horizontal. Then do a banana turnover and allow the device to pinwheel underneath the non-throwing hand. Then we can set up a counterweight in the throwing hand to help the device land properly. To do this, you can just put the string in between the middle and ring finger of the throwing hand so that the counterweight can come up between them. Take the throwing hand at this time and flex it down as much as you can to get the spinning top.

When the counterweight is in the right position, take the device while it is pinwheeling and lift it up, move the throwing hand underneath, and then drop the hand a bit to cushion the device fall a bit. Here you will notice how the yo-yo is grinding on the dice. Once it is spinning on the counterweight, let it spin for as long as you can. To dismount off this trick, just hop up the device and then bring it to an undermount.

Helicopter

To make this particular trick a bit easier, you will want to break it into two parts. The first is to do a trapeze. From here, you can choke up on your counterweight. It can help if you pinch the string a bit. Then throw the device so it goes in a counter-clockwise motion above the device. For the second part, you will throw a trapeze again. From here, bring both of the hands together and do some forward rolls in between these two hands. If you want to, you can also allow a few wraps around your hand as you are doing the rolls.

The Bee's knees

You will want to start out doing a trapeze and then move to the 360. From here, catch the counterweight in your throwing hand, about halfway down. You want this to get right under the thigh and tap right at the bottom and then leave it there. Then you can do a reverse bee sting. To do this, bring the yo-yo to an undermount. Then, rather than pulling the device off the string, you will see that this makes it come off your leg. Instead, pinch the string right about the yo-yo and then move the hand around so the string can stay on the thigh.

Then, you can really exaggerate the outward motion of the reverse bee sting so that the yo-yo leaves the thigh. Then do the pinching and unrolling motion again so you end up in an undermount. Then pinch the two strings with the middle finger and thumb. Pull out the hand to bring the weight back to the throwing hand thigh. Roll the yo-yo with the throwing hand side once. As it comes around, catch the yo-yo.

From here, we want to dismount the yo-yo. Let it have time to come all the way around, swinging at the end of the string. Land the yo-yo into an under the leg trapeze and then into a bee sting while dropping the throwing hand foot. Catch the yo-yo when it is in an undermount and then perform a bind.

Chapter 5: Using Both Hands

In this chapter, we are going to take some time to look at a few tricks that you can use that work with two hands. The other tricks focused mainly on one-handed tricks to help you move the yo-yo around, but now it is time to expand on this a bit and see what can happen. Some of the two-handed tricks that we are going to explore include:

The Sidewinder

This trick will need you to start out with a good sleeper. As it sleeps, you can move the device to either the right or the left hand to help either loosen or tighten the string. When the device gets to a good height, you can start to pull it over to yourself so that it rises and evens out with your hand level. Once you are here, you can use both of your hands to work on some of the other tricks.

Two-handed around the world

You will need to grab two yo-yos and then do the around the world trick with both hands. There are various techniques and variations that you can choose to go with. To do both of these at the same time, make sure that one of the hands starts before the other so you don't end up with a collision as you go.

Beat around the world

This is a trick that had you use around the world and it is best when you learn how to cross your normal throw hand over the non-throw hand first. This will feel more comfortable and when you are ready, you can then progress to the next level where the opposite hand starts to cross the yo-yo hand.

The Butterfly

This is going to include around the worlds crisscrossing each other across the body rather than doing it at your sides. This is going to make the butterfly shape. You want to make sure that the two hands are at different heights a little bit to make sure that there is better control. The planes of the devices need to be a bit different or you will end up with them colliding.

Sherlock and Dr. Watson

The idea here is that the hand that is considered weaker or the usual non-throwing hand will do the same motion over and over again as your Dr. Watson hand. The other side is going to do whatever trick that you want while the non-throwing hand does a simple loop or something similar. This helps you to work on your levels of control.

Milk the cow

This is just hop the fence, but you are going to use both hands. The name is going to come from the movement of your hands when you perform this cow because it does look like you are milking a cow. Just go through and use the techniques that we talked about with hop the fence, but use it with both hands. As you continue, you will want the strings to cross and have loops that are alternating. This is a trick known as cattle crossing.

Basic long spin wraps

To do this one, you need to have your usual nonthrowing hand out. Then take the device and throw it across the wrist section so that it is able to fall between your opposite arm and the string. You can then create a wrap on top of your arm, using the dominant arm and unwrap it with the non-throw arm. From here, create a wrap and then get out of the wrap. You can then expand this by turning the body so it has the effect that you are going to throw the yo-yo behind you.

Two-handed vertical punches

This trick is going to involve milk the cow but will be more vertical. You will have a little fight with gravity with this one and the speed you get when you perform this trick will help a lot with this issue. You will need to work on your straight up throws a bit and then adjust the angle of your hands when you throw to help you discover the right angle that seems to work for you. Sitting back in a recliner when you practice this one can help quite a bit too.

Snap wind

To do this one, you will want to hold the yo-yo between the middle finger and thumb, pushing the yo-yo with the help of your thumb. Make it go upward a bit so it sits there while the middle finger works to put the spin on the device. Once the spin is going well, you can try this out with your finger. Just allow the string to hang out and give it a snap. Try to make sure that the string doesn't get really twisted here and it will be a lot easier.

Sidewinder

To get started with this one, you will want to throw a good sleeper. When the yo-yo is sleeping, you will need to move the device over to the left or the right, depending on whether the string should be together or looser. You just need to push off it really slowly. When your device gets to the right height, you will take your hand and pull this towards yourself a bit. This causes the yo-yo to get a bit higher and the goal is to get it to become level with the hand. If that happens, then the string will spin out. Once you master this on one hand, you will then be able to add on a second hand as well.

Windshield wipers

Now we are going to take a look at how to do some windshield wipers. To do this, you can just throw to one side, let the device swing across, then do a regen on the other side, swinging it back to the other side. Repeat these steps over and over again. You want the device to stay completely straight down and up throughout the whole trick to make it easier to do more repetitions and to add in more consistency.

Chapter 6: Making it More Advanced

When you get here, you have spent some time practicing some of the other tricks for a bit and you are ready to make things a bit more advanced. We are going to take a look at some tricks that are a bit more difficult and it will take some dedication to make these happen. But the results are so worth it. Some of the tricks that we are going to take a look at here include:

Velvet mount

This mount is simply taking each yo-yo and throwing them down before raising them up with the opposing finger so they end up on the string. Just throw down the device, the opposite hand first and then lift it a bit to get it back up on the string. The throwing hand is going to push into the string and place the yo-yo on the string as well.

Each one is on its own string and you can then drop them without worrying about the strings tangling at all.

Velvet rolls

For this trick, you will have to start out with a velvet mount and then while you have the mount down, you will flip both of the devices round to the back, doing it one at a time. You can choose to do this as many times as you want before bringing the devices back to your hands. You can make this work a bit easier by keeping the arms by your sides and the fingers straight.

Gunslinger

This trick has two methods when it comes to performing it. Both the inside and outside tracks can be used. Simply place the index finger on the inside of the string and then do a quick whip motion. You will want to catch the device with the string that is furthest away from you. The motion is going to be similar to the drawing motion in old westerns. To whip the device to the outside, just place the finger on the outside of the string and then repeat this motion.

Assisted barrel rolls

You will start out this trick with the same method that you got with a normal barrel roll, but rather than doing the trick over the free hand's finger, you are going to do it with the other yo-yo. You can start this trick with a split bottom mount and then start doing a barrel roll with your throw hand. Keep the hands aligned as much as you can to make the trick a bit easier. If you move the hands from each other, this leads to a turn in the device that can ruin the results of the trick.

Assisted Mach 5

This one is just like the normal Mach 5 but you will do it over the opposite hand's yo-yo rather than the hand. Start out this trick with a barrel roll and then you can take the yo-yo from your non-throwing hand and have it go over the other one before going under. Then you can pull on the strings tight and do a Mach 5, keeping the hands straight as much as possible.

Blue line mount

This one is going to need a few steps to make it happen but it is well worth the work. The first stage is doing a split bottom mount that will be performed over the wrist of your free hand. You should try to get the move with just one throw. Then finish with a flip forward so you are gripping the string.

For the second stage, begin with the throw on the free hand. Then take the other hand and do a mount over the wrist. A flip forward is next and then take the strings in your fingers. This is going to allow you to pull the hound out and do a split bottom mount with the free hand's device. At this point, you can do a forward flip of both devices before dropping the dismount, making a circular motion and undoing the strings.

Incendio

To start this trick, take the throwing hand and throw a breakaway. Then this needs to be mounted over the index finger and wrist of the opposite hand. You can then unmount and use the momentum that you have going and end up with a world tour, which is simply an around the world that is done at the front of the body. The throwing hand needs to do a Gunslinger that turns into a world tour. This is basically so that the hands start to do the same trick going in the same direction as well.

Basic off string wind

Take your string and make sure that it is lying across the top of the device. Pinch the string with your thumb and then let the device wind up as it normally does removing the pinch halfway through and winding it right onto the device.

Basic throw for off string

The difference that comes with this and the basic throw of a normal throw is that you need to do a different angle to make sure that you can catch this one. Once you get the device back onto the string, you can do a few twists in order to get rid of the tilts that may come in.

Toss and catch

The easiest method to use to do this one is to take the top string and move the hands apart just a little bit. If you want the device to come outside your string, you simply need to twist the throw arm a bit. This ensures that the string is able to move away and the device won't run into it at all.

Forward mount trick

For this trick, you want to take the device and throw it over your free hand. You can then use the hand to catch the string and get it to move up. This allows you to get the throw hand to go below the device, which can make it easier for you to catch later on when needed.

Leg orbits

Orbits are a neat trick to do because it is when the yo-yo goes around the body, any part. With this one, we are getting the device to go around your leg. The easiest method to use for this one is to take the leg over the device and then swing the device back and forth. Once the device reaches your non-throwing hand, toss it over your leg so that you are able to catch it on the other side. You may want to make sure that you do well with whipping action before you try it with the leg.

Underhand whip

This is a trick that you want to start out with pinching the string. The pinching motion should be done with the throwing hand. Then you can part the strings to ensure that the top string is on the inside of your body. From here, you can pop the device to the outside of your body. To get the whip done, you can do a circular motion with the elbow in the air and the palm of the working hand down. What this does is send the string under the device, allowing it to catch back on the string again.

Cast whip

This trick is basically an overhand whip but it is going to need some more height for the device. You will whip your string past the yo-yo and then catch it in the floating string. To get that floating string to work, you can bring the hands down with the string. Then the floating motion will be done and you just need to make sure that you catch the yo-yo on the string.

Recaptures

This is something that you can consider doing each time that you land your yo-yo. By placing your hand either under or over the device, you are doing this move. You can finish with the arms crossed. To get the dismount done, you just need to flip the device and uncross, which gets you back to the starting mount.

String your counterweight

If your counterweight has a hole that goes through it, then it is time to take the loop that you created and pass it on through the hole. You can then take the slipknot end of your string and make sure it is pulled tight until the string is able to tighten around the counterweight.

Hold the counterweight

From here, you will want to make a shape of a gun using the throwing hand and then cradle the string above the weight. You will need to use three fingers to make this work. There should now be a counterweight close to the little finger here. The yo-yo is then going to rest on the middle finger. If you close up the thumb, the yo-yo is going to be right in your hand.

360 trick

You will start out this one with the trapeze. Stop here to adjust the proportions of your string.

You will need about ¾ of the string to be above the finger. Now, take the throwing hand back out so that you can get the device to swing. As it is swinging, you can release the counterweight and make a motion that is circular with your free hand. This is a motion that will ensure that the string from the counterweight is going to touch your device and that ends the trick.

Release of the double or nothing

This is a simple trick for you to perform. You just do a double or nothing. You can then release the counterweight when you separate the hands from each other. You may need to play around with how fast you separate out the hands to ensure that the counterweight is going to behave the way that it needs to here.

Chain Wraps

This trick is going to involve four around the worlds, with two of them at the front of the body and then the other two in the back. You can start this trick with a strong breakaway and then you let the device go all around before sticking your arm out, allowing the device to go right underneath. From here, you will use the arm to push it behind you. Once you are comfortable with doing this, you can then throw an around the world behind the back before pulling it in front of you. When the yo-yo does come to the front, you should bend your arm as if you want to put the hand on your hip, to make it easier to get the device back to the front. Repeat as often as you would like.

Arm wrap

For this trick, you want to do an around the world but don't let it go all the way around you. Instead, you will keep your arm out so that the device can wrap up under the arm. From this point, the momentum is going to carry it over and you can then catch it in your hand on the outside of the shoulder. You can pinch the string to help keep the device in control as it spins. Then do three more circles, going in the same direction with this device. So you will do one, then you turn, step through and then let it come right out from under the arm.

Warp drive

For the warp drive, you will need to do a loop that goes into around the world and then back to looping again. There isn't a ton of technique to make this work, but it can be a nice one to utilize because it brings together a few different tricks and you combine them into one. When you go into the around the world, make sure that you add in a bit of cushion when you throw it out so that the device can sleep and go around. Do not let the yo-yo slow down as it comes in front of you or the trick will have to be restarted.

The stall

The idea behind this trick is that you are going to go through and slow the device down a bit so that it is close to stopping or actually stops before throwing it back out again. This helps you to go from one trick to the other without needing to catch the device each time. The easiest way for you to do this stall is to start out using a normal throw. But instead of letting it go straight down, throw it forward a bit to get it to swing around towards you. Then you can catch it back. But instead of catching it, you should stall. Just bring the hand back with the motion of the device to help it slow down a bit. This cushions the throw a little bit so you get better results.

Guillotine

The next trick that we are going to take a look at is known as the Guillotine. When you are ready to do this trick, you will want to throw a strong breakaway. And during the breakaway, you need to let the yo-yo go right around the neck. Before it has time to come around and hit you in the face, it is time to turn the body and stand upright. This makes it sits so that the device can pass around the side of the head and across your body. When it does this, you can catch the device and go on to the next trick.

Leg wrap trap

To do the leg wrap trap, you will throw the yo-yo out in a strong around the world but make sure it is going sideways. As it is going around, you can take a step forward on the side where you are holding the yo-yo. Let the device go right between the legs. You will then want the device to continue around in a circular motion while also stepping forward with the other leg. The device will need to pass right through from there. To end this trick, you will need to land a trapeze.

Punching bags

The punching bag is basically going to be a looping trick. But instead of going through and looping in the normal direction, the punching bag is going to head in the opposite direction. The first thing to do to get this mastered is to get hop the fence down. But instead of doing the hop the fence straight down, you will do it straight forward.

The fountain

This is one that you can do together with the punching bags and hop the fence. This one is going to have the same movements as the other two, but you will go straight up rather than down or in front of you. After you try this trick out a few times, you will be able to do a combination of hop the fence, punching bags, and fountain to come up with a great trick.

Pendulum wrap

To start with this trick, you will need to start out with a trapeze. Then you can go into a basic stall. Right after it begins to stall, you will want to take the pointer finger on the throwing hand and hook it right in front of the string on the counterweight. This drapes the string over the finger and the finger points right to you. When the counterweight is stalled, you will want it to swing in the other direction so you can get it over to the gap in the front of the two strings on your opposite hand. You should catch the device with the palm up and then drop the string on the pointer finger to get the yo-yo over into a trapeze.

Going from here, you will want to pinch the trapeze string above the device with the thumb and the pointer finger on the non-throwing hand. Then set up the string with the pointer finger hooked inside. Swing the counterweight into the gap again, but instead of catching it, you can let it go around to the front of your two strings. Continue this momentum of the counterweight around the yo-yo around a second time, then catch your device before dropping the string from the pointer finger. Now, you should do an undermount and then perform a bind to finish.

The Nunchuck

To work on this trick, you will start out with the split bottom mount. Then just pull out the opposite hand. You will do a trick that is known as the keychain but the hand is open. What this does is allows you to let go of your device so it can unwrap. When it is unwrapping, the momentum should carry this around to get everything around the shoulder. Then grab the device, get some momentum and pull the yo-yo so it goes around the shoulder. Bring it back to your hand to finish the trick.

The umbrella

You will start this one with a breakaway. Then take the left hand and have it hold up the device. Then swing it across the body. As the device comes towards you, you can then pull down on it to make sure it launches across the body. This helps you get the right momentum to work on this. From here, you can release the device so that it slides over to the left hand. You are back in your original position and can keep going through the same steps over again.

Bee sting

To get started with the bee sting, you can start with the trapeze. Stop and check the string proportions. Then you can take the throwing hand and make sure that the string that is above the throwing hand is not more than twice as long as what is underneath. Once the proportions are right, do a 360. But instead of catching the device, you will instead stick out the middle finger and hop the yo-yo over so the counterweight string can come under and hook to the device like with a half bee sting.

You can also stop and not catch the device, allowing it to continue before doing a clockwise circular motion with the non-throwing hand. This will add in an extra revolution to the device and an extra pinwheel to the yo-yo. This can help you get the device back to a trapeze and then you can do the undermount to perform a bind.

The reverse bee sting

To do this one, you will want to bring in the device close to the pointer finger on the non-throwing hand. If the yo-yo gets too close to the counterweight, this trick is harder to do. Going from here, you will stick out the middle finger and get the yo-yo to hop over the middle finger before bringing it into an undermount. As the yo-yo goes to the undermount, make sure that you loosen the

106

grip a bit and then bring out the opposite hand, right as the device starts to touch the bottom of the string.

The counterweight of the device will then leave your hand to start an arc. When it gets to fifteen degrees above parallel to the ground, you will want to stick out the pointer finger and then make a crescent motion with that hand, bringing it back to the throwing hand side. The counterweight will start to come under the device so that it can land on the trapeze.

The Keychain or One-Finger spin

The keychain is something that you can do with either a side or a front mount. To do it with a side mount, you will then let the string fall off the non-throwing hand so that all of it is on the yo-yo hand. Then you will allow the device to go in the same direction, with it already spinning. When you stop the device, you will either take the hand then

The Yo-Yo Prodigies

pull the string off or you can do a dismount to flip the device in the opposite direction.

Conclusion

This guidebook is the ultimate guide that you need to take your skills with the yo-yo from beginner to expert in no time. This is a great hobby to work with, one that can help you have fun for hours with such a simple tool. It may take some time to learn how to do the different tricks that we talk about in this guidebook, but before long, you will be able to get the yo-yo device to behave the way that you want while also impressing your friends and family.

This guidebook has yo-yo tricks that work for people of all talent and skill levels. If you have never even used a yo-yo, there are some tips and tricks that are there for you. If you want to learn some tricks that help you to impress others and put on a show, then there are a few tricks that are available too. There are tricks to do a show off to others, tricks that can help advance your skills, tricks for two hands, and so much more.

If you want to learn how to do more tricks with a yo-yo and expand out your skills, then this guidebook has all the information that you need to get started!

One Final Thing...

Thank for making it through to the end of *Yo-Yo Tricks*, let's hope you master some fun and cool yo-yo tricks.

Did You Enjoy the Book?

If you did, please let us know by leaving a review on AMAZON. Review let Amazon know that we are creating quality material for children. Even a few words and ratings would go a long way. We would like to thank you in advance for your time.

If you have any comments, or suggestions for improvement for other books, we would love to hear from and you and can contact us at theyoyoprodigies@bmccpublishing.com

Your comments are greatly valued and the book have already been revised and improved as a result of helpful suggestions from readers.

Made in the USA
Monee, IL
03 December 2019

17799168R00067